W0254416

For Penny – H. G.

For my family and friends – R. M.

First published 2026 by Two Hoots, an imprint of Pan Macmillan
The Smithson, 6 Briset Street, London EC1M 5NR
EU representative: Macmillan Publishers Ireland Limited, 1st Floor,
The Liffey Trust Centre, 117–126 Sheriff Street Upper, Dublin 1, D01 YC43

Associated companies throughout the world
www.panmacmillan.com
ISBN 978-1-0350-2424-7

1 3 5 7 9 8 6 4 2
A CIP catalogue record for this book is available from the British Library.
Printed in China
The illustrations in this book were created using digital media.
www.twohootsbooks.com

Henry Gee
Raxenne Maniquiz

THE WONDER OF LIFE ON EARTH

The story of our planet, evolution and you

TWO HOOTS

Contents

Timeline

HADEAN EON 4.6–4 bya

ARCHAEAN EON 4–2.5 bya

PALAEOPROTEROZOIC ERA 2.5–1.6 bya

MESOPROTEROZOIC ERA 1.6–1 bya

Tonian Period 1 bya – 720 mya

Cryogenian Period 720–635 mya

Ediacaran Period 635–541 mya

NEOPROTEROZOIC ERA 1 bya – 539 mya

PROTEROZOIC EON 2.5 bya – 539 mya

Cambrian Period 541–485 mya

Ordovician Period 485–444 mya

Silurian Period 444–419 mya

Devonian Period 419–359 mya

Carboniferous Period 359–299 mya

Permian Period 299–252 mya

PALAEOZOIC ERA 539–252 mya

Billion years ago – bya · Million years ago – mya

PHANEROZOIC EON 539 mya – now

CENOZOIC ERA 66 mya – now

Quaternary Period 2.6 mya – now

Holocene Epoch 11,000 years ago – now

Pleistocene Epoch 2.6 mya – 11,000 years ago

Neogene Period 23–2.6 mya

Pliocene Epoch 5.3–2.6 mya

Miocene Epoch 23–5.3 mya

Palaeogene Period 66–23 mya

Oligocene Epoch 34–23 mya

Eocene Epoch 56–34 mya

Palaeocene Epoch 66–56 mya

MESOZOIC ERA 252–66 mya

Cretaceous Period 145–66 mya

Jurassic Period 201–145 mya

Triassic Period 252–201 mya

Evolution

In the nineteenth century, a naturalist called Charles Darwin developed a theory about life on Earth: the theory of evolution.

During a voyage around the world between 1831 and 1836, Darwin was astonished by the variety of life on Earth. There were so many different species of birds, plants, and other life forms. He wondered why. Could one species be descended from another species, like children from parents?

Back at home in England, Darwin started thinking about how farmers often bred together very woolly sheep, or cows that produced a lot of milk. A lamb whose parents were both very woolly would be more likely to grow up to be woolly as well. This was called artificial selection. Properties of parents could be passed on to the child – or inherited. And, with time, those features could be enhanced even more.

Darwin himself demonstrated the theory by breeding fancy pigeons. He showed that the common pigeon could be bred over time to develop a dramatic collar of feathers, or to grow a longer neck.

Darwin wondered whether something similar might be happening in the wild, too – a process he called natural selection. This time, it wouldn't be farmers doing the selecting, but the natural environment around us.

Take the frogs in my garden pond. Hundreds of tadpoles are born, but only a few will live to become frogs. These will be the tadpoles that are best at avoiding being eaten. If one tadpole has a particularly strong tail that helps it escape, then when it has its own offspring, those tadpoles will also be more likely to have strong tails.

The animals that are most successful at breeding and surviving are the ones that pass on their traits. Over millions of years, the traits that are passed down will change in tiny ways, leading eventually to bigger changes – even whole new species. This is called evolution.

In Darwin's day, people thought that the Earth was only a few thousand years old at most. But scientists gradually discovered that the Earth is billions of years old – long enough to create a stage for evolution's great drama. This is why there are so many different creatures on Earth today.

The early Earth was a hostile place. There was no oxygen in the air. It was very hot. Imagine yourself on the early Earth – you could never predict the amazing range of life forms that would eventually evolve on this small, rocky planet.

Fossils

A word about fossils.

Fossils are the remains of ancient life forms that were buried soon after death and have become preserved in rocks. The earliest fossils are the remains of cyanobacteria preserved in stromatolites (see page 20).

Most fossils are formed from the hard parts of living things, such as shells, teeth and bones, because the soft parts usually rot away over time. This is why the dinosaurs you see in museums are skeletons.

Sometimes, though, softer parts such as skin, feathers and hair are preserved too, allowing a more complete picture of what ancient life was like.

Fossils are rare, and often hard to understand. But without them, we would know very much less about the history of life on Earth, and nothing at all about the vast range of incredible organisms that died out long ago.

Thanks to fossils, we can begin to imagine what some of these long-vanished creatures looked like. Without fossils, for example, we'd know nothing at all about the amazingly weird animals of the Ediacaran Period (page 36); the Cambrian creatures found in the Burgess Shale (page 40); or the wonders of the Triassic Period (page 56). And imagine a world in which we knew nothing about dinosaurs . . . if you can.

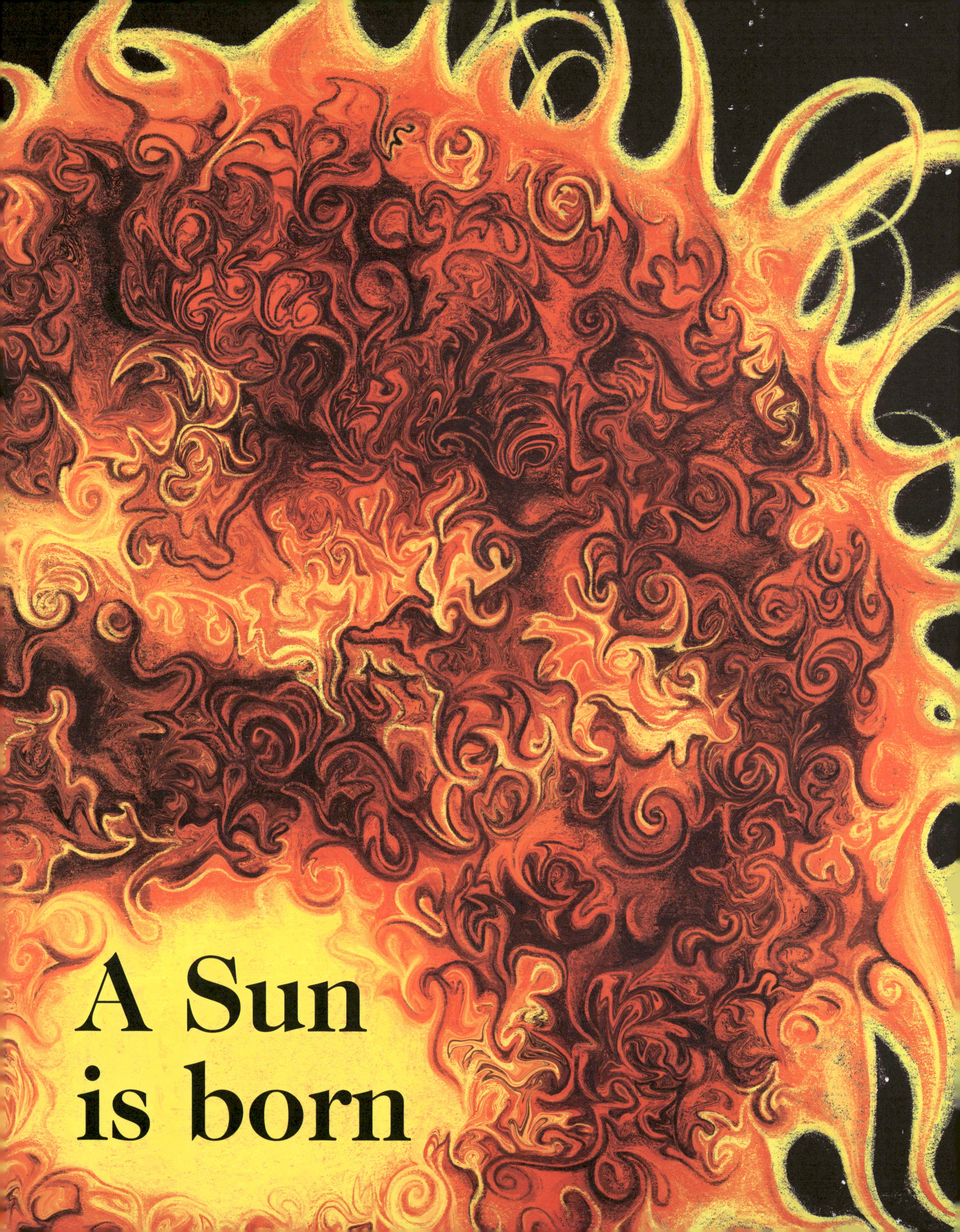
A Sun
is born

Long ago, a huge star was burning. It was many times bigger than our own Sun.

Nuclear fusion is what makes stars burn. It is fuelled by gases which are squashed under great pressure. This creates huge amounts of energy, which we see as light. Nuclear fusion is the heart of every glowing star you see in the night sky. But it does more than make stars shine. It also creates enough energy to stop a huge star from collapsing under its own weight.

This particular star was very old, and had been burning for so long that it was running out of fuel. The process of nuclear fusion was beginning to slow and fade. The star gradually began to produce less light, and less heat. It turned from white, to yellow, to a deep, sullen red.

Eventually, the fuel ran out. After millions of years of shining, the great star gave in to its own weight, and collapsed. This took a split second. There was an explosion so violent that it briefly lit up the whole galaxy – a supernova.

Materials created in the star's dying moments – such as silicon, carbon, oxygen, iron and uranium – surfed the wave made by the supernova.

After travelling through space for millions of years, the wave of stardust disturbed a cloud rich in dust, gas and ice. The centre of this cloud became so hot and dense that nuclear fusion began, creating heat and light. A new star was born – the Sun.

Circling the Sun, the rest of the cloud of dust, gas and ice came together over a period of millions of years to form planets. All this happened more than 4.6 billion years ago.

One of those planets was our Earth.

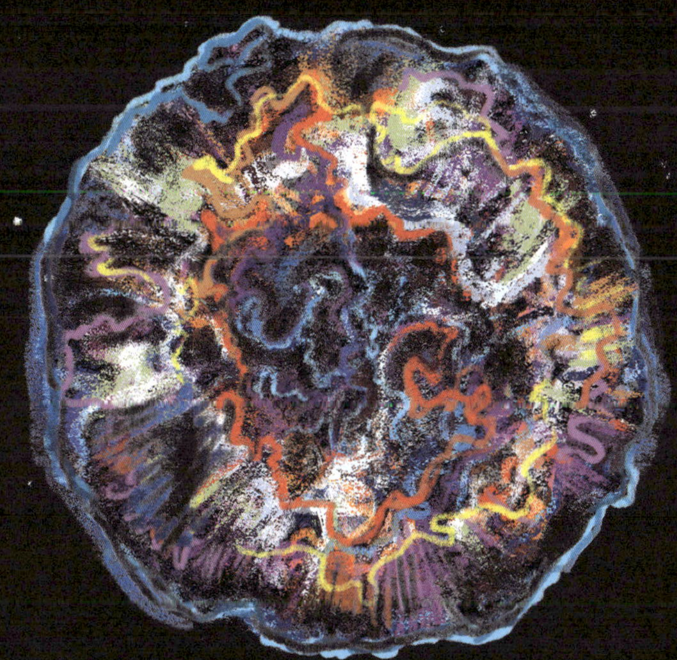

Planet Volcano

The Earth is a huge mass of rock made of layers, like a cake. At the core is a ball of hot, liquid metal.

Around the core is a layer of molten rock, called the mantle. It is thousands of kilometres thick and the consistency of warm treacle, forever kept moving by the heat from the core below. The rocky outer layer is only a few kilometres thick. This is the crust, which moves as it is caught and nudged by the mantle below. This movement breaks the crust into separate pieces, called tectonic plates. Earthquakes can happen when these plates rub against each other.

Volcanoes are places where hot, molten rock (or lava) gushes through the Earth's crust to the surface.

The infant Earth was very different from the peaceful planet we know today. It was a ball of magma, constantly bombarded by other, smaller planets. One of them, a planet the size of Mars, struck the young Earth. The crust was ripped off into space. For a while, our Earth was surrounded by a ring of rocks, like the planet Saturn today. These rocks came together to form our Moon.

Around the Earth is a thin layer of gases called the atmosphere. The atmosphere of the early Earth was very different from the atmosphere we breathe today. For a start, there was no oxygen. Instead, there were gases such as carbon dioxide and methane. The air was foggy with water vapour.

After millions of years, the Earth cooled enough for the water above to become liquid and fall as rain. It rained for millions of years – enough to make the first oceans. Icy comets fell from space, adding more water.

Once a ball of fiery magma, the Earth became a world of water. Magma spewed out into the ocean from underwater volcanoes. It was volcanoes that built the first land.

In the depths of the earliest oceans, it was jets of volcano-heated water squirting from cracks in the crust that would fuel the first life.

Bubbles

The early Earth was a violent place.

Among all the volcanoes and comets, life began, around 4.1 billion years ago. Small membranes like soap bubbles stretched across tiny holes in rocks on the ocean floor. Boiling-hot water filled with particles of iron, and sulphur from deep in the Earth gushed out of cracks in the crust.

Cooling and slowing as they met the cold seawater, streams of water dropped their cargo into the rock holes. These holes became tiny caves of peace and order, protected by their membranes from the chaos outside.

Membranes are barriers. They separate an inside from an outside. The earliest membranes were leaky, letting some things in and out. Gradually, the insides of these little caves became very different from the world outside.

At first, the membranes protected the rock holes, meaning atoms could mix together and create more complicated substances. These substances included proteins, which make up the bodies of living things; and deoxyribonucleic acid, or DNA.

DNA is a key ingredient of life: it contains instructions for making proteins. These instructions are called genes and they are passed down from one life form to another. DNA and genes are the building blocks of life.

The soap-bubble membranes would sometimes float off into the sea, each a package of proteins and DNA. These bubbles were the first living things.

Evolution had begun.

DNA (deoxyribonucleic acid)

Cyanobacteria

The Sun, Earth and Moon formed around 4.6 billion years ago. By 4.1 billion years ago, life had appeared.

The early Earth and Moon were bombarded by large meteorites from outer space. These collisions formed the dark areas on the Moon. By about 3.7 billion years ago, life had migrated from the ocean depths to the sunlit surface of the water.

Some living beings were big enough to see with the naked eye. Masses of tiny life forms called cyanobacteria (or sometimes 'blue-green algae') began to clump together.

Although each individual **cyanobacterium** (1) can only be seen with a microscope, when cyanobacteria get together they form long threads and tough sheets that are easy to see.

1. Cyanobacterium 2. Stromatolite

The first cyanobacteria became lawns on the seafloor. Waves and storms covered them with sand, then more cyanobacteria grew on top. These, too, were then covered with sand. And so it went on, creating layered mounds of cyanobacteria and sand that we call stromatolites (2).

By 3.4 billion years ago, stromatolites had formed the first reefs – huge living structures that could have been seen from space.

Today, stromatolites only survive in a few places that are too salty for other living things. But cyanobacteria form bright green scum on ponds and lakes all over the world to this day.

Although now there are not many left, stromatolite reefs were the only life on Earth for 3 billion years.

2

Carbon

Carbon warms the Earth. The Earth absorbs carbon. Without carbon, the Earth would be uninhabitably cold.

LAND

The Earth's crust is divided into tectonic plates. These rub up against, slide past and burrow underneath one another, causing earthquakes and volcanic eruptions. Volcanoes poking above the surface of the sea formed the first land. Eventually, these islands melded together to create continents.

SKY

Early Earth was surrounded by many gases, including carbon dioxide. When the first land formed, rocks began to absorb carbon dioxide. These carbon-rich rocks are broken up into grains by rain and wind: a process called weathering. Eventually, carbon grains wash into the ocean, then are absorbed into the mantle. Volcanic eruptions send carbon up into the atmosphere once again.

Balance

But too much carbon dioxide released into the atmosphere by human activity is impacting the climate, making it harder for human life to exist.

HOT

Carbon dioxide keeps the Earth warm. It is clear, so it lets sunlight hit the Earth, but traps heat coming off the surface. This is called the greenhouse effect. Fuels like oil and coal send extra carbon dioxide into the atmosphere, making the Earth hotter. This is why people are worried about the use of these fossil fuels. They are making the Earth warmer and changing its climate.

COLD

The Sun is getting hotter. Millions of years ago, the Sun was not as hot as it is today. If it were not for the greenhouse effect, the Earth would have frozen long ago. At times, more carbon dioxide was absorbed by the land than came out of volcanoes. The amount of carbon dioxide in the atmosphere fell, the greenhouse effect weakened, and the Earth got colder. Sometimes the entire planet froze for millions of years.

Sun and Air

Without the sun, there could be no life on earth. But it can also be deadly.

When the earliest life forms migrated from the dark depths of the ocean towards the surface, they faced a new challenge – sunlight. Today, a form of oxygen in the atmosphere called ozone absorbs harmful ultraviolet rays from the Sun. But 3 billion years ago there was almost no oxygen in the atmosphere, and no ozone. Early life forms were killed by the sunlight.

Some living things developed ways to absorb the Sun's energy – a kind of inbuilt sunscreen. Once absorbed, the sun's energy could be put to work. Life forms used the sun's energy to drive chemical reactions that converted carbon dioxide into food, a process called photosynthesis. Plants do this today.

But plants need more than just carbon dioxide and sunlight to drive photosynthesis – they need a fuel. Early life forms used iron and sulphur-based chemicals as fuel. But the best fuel is the easiest to find – water. But there was a catch. Photosynthesis created a colourless, odourless gas that reacts with almost anything it touches. It is one of the most deadly substances on Earth. That substance is oxygen, or O_2.

To almost all life, which had evolved in an oxygen-free world, O_2 was a deadly poison. Oxygen released by photosynthesis wiped out a huge amount of life on Earth. Many creatures ceased to exist, becoming extinct. This was the first of many mass extinctions in Earth's history.

Rocks from that time show bands of deep red, where oxygen turned iron minerals into rust. At the same time, volcanic activity and the formation of land caused weathering, which is when the land absorbs carbon dioxide. This sucked the warming blanket of carbon dioxide from the atmosphere, sparking an Ice Age.

The Earth was completely covered in ice for 300 million years: the longest Ice Age in Earth's history. But this also sparked evolution into a frenzy of activity. Life forms that could tolerate oxygen flourished. Seaweeds and some simple animals began to evolve.

Bacteria

Bacteria can be found deep in the Earth, at the edge of space, underneath ice, and in boiling-hot springs.

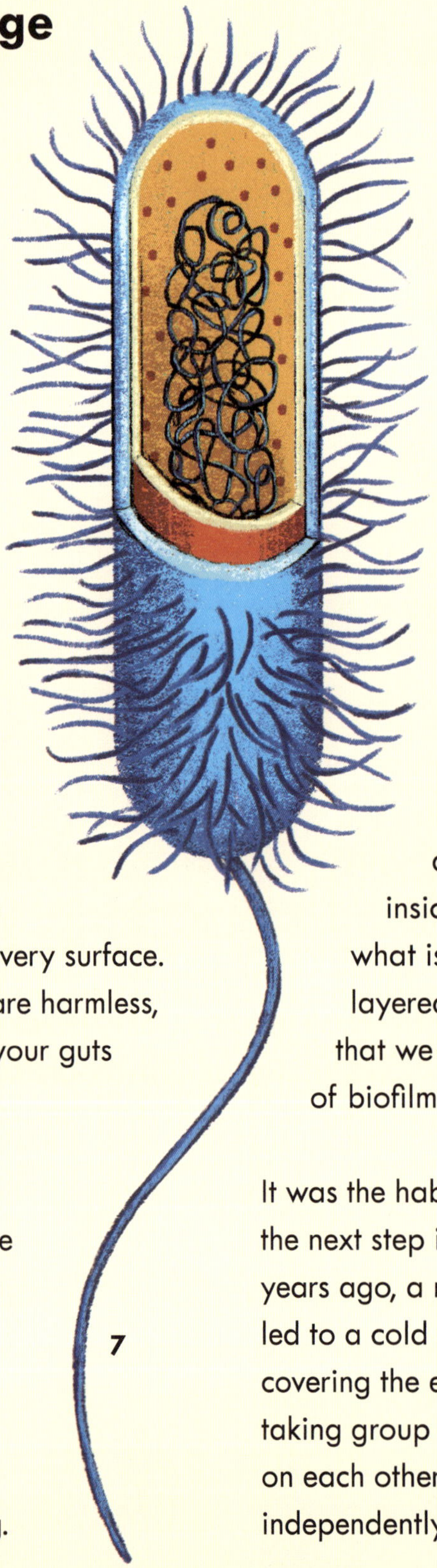

Bacteria evolved more than 3.5 billion years ago and they remain the most common life form on Earth, even though each individual (or 'bacterium') is far too small to see without a powerful microscope.

There are as many bacteria in your body as your body has cells (a cell is one of the tiny particles that make up every living thing). They swarm over every surface. Although some cause diseases, most are harmless, and some – like the millions living in your guts – are vital for health.

Imagine a lentil sitting on a watermelon. That's the same difference in size as a bacterium compared with one of your own cells.

Despite their tiny size, bacteria have a fantastic ability to live almost anywhere and digest almost anything.

There are bacteria that can digest petroleum and some can even live in waste from nuclear power plants that would be deadly to you or me.

Bacteria love to flock together. Different types live in communities with each other, because what is waste to one species is food for another. Sometimes different bacteria live inside a single, slimy envelope and create what is called a biofilm. Stromatolites (the layered mounds of sand and cyanobacteria that we met in a previous chapter) are a kind of biofilm.

It was the habit of bacteria living together that led to the next step in evolution. Between 2.4 and 2.1 billion years ago, a massive change in Earth's atmosphere led to a cold snap that lasted 300 million years, covering the entire planet in ice. Bacteria reacted by taking group living even further, becoming so reliant on each other that they could no longer function independently.

The first true cells were born.

7

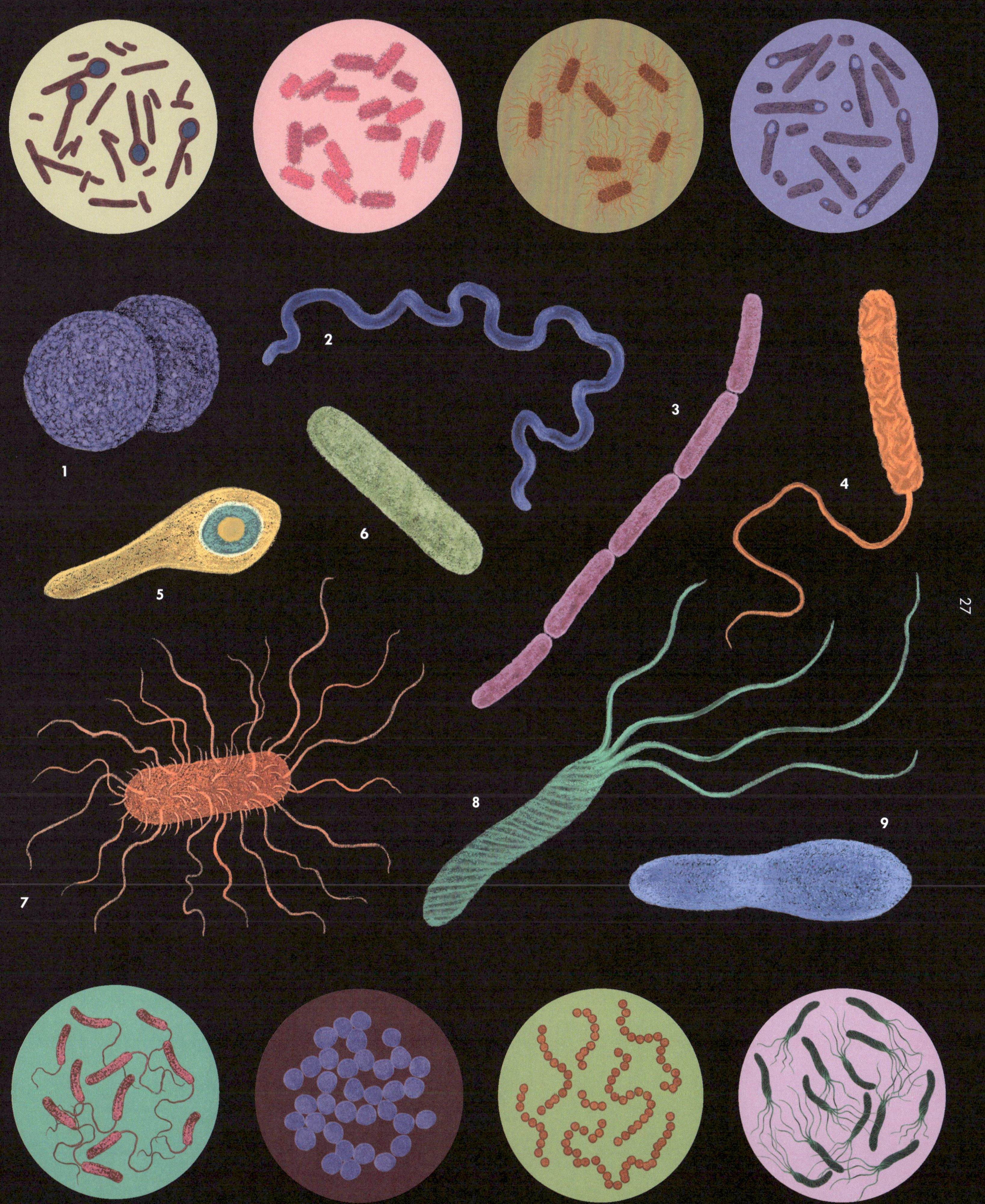

1. Streptococcus pneumoniae 2. Treponema pallidum 3. Streptobacillus moniliformis 4. Vibrio cholerae 5. Clostridium tetani 6. Legionella pneumophila 7. Salmonella typhimurium 8. Helicobacter pylori 9. Clostridium botulinum

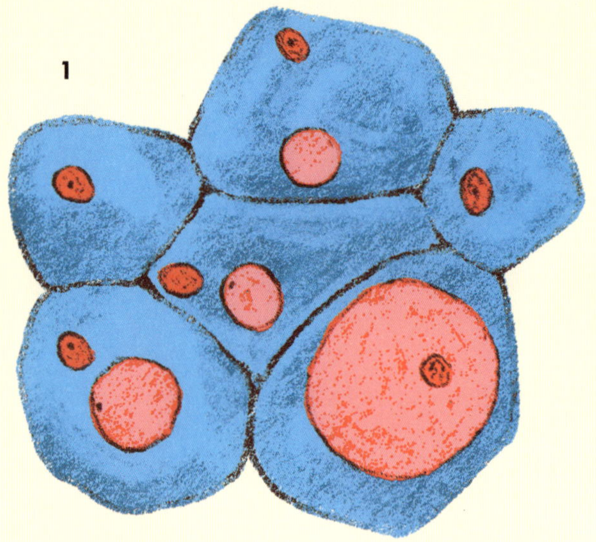

1. Plant cell
2. Warnowiid
3. Amoeba
4. Radiolarian

Every animal and plant is made of millions of tiny **cells** (1). Each cell is made of many parts. At the centre of the cell is a blob called the nucleus, rich in the genetic material DNA. This is the cell's library, containing all the information to make more cells. Everything is contained inside a membrane, not so different from the soap-bubble membranes of the earliest living things.

Your cells are very different from bacteria. As well as being much smaller than cells like yours, bacteria have no clear internal structure. There is DNA, but it floats free. There is no nucleus. Everything is in the same space, all together.

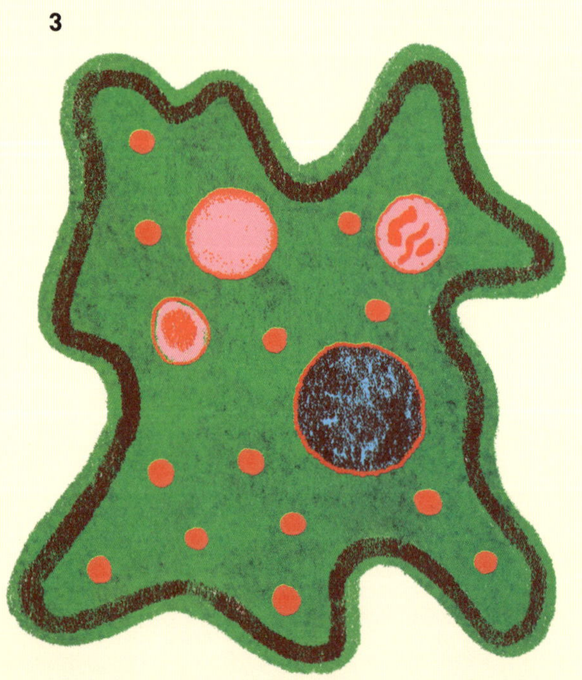

Some creatures consist of one single cell – these are called protists. Being made of a single cell doesn't mean that protists cannot be complicated. Some rare protists, the **warnowiids** (2), have tiny eyes, amazingly like our own – which help them hunt for other protists.

Protists include **amoeba** (3) and **paramecium** you might find in a garden pond; blooms of **diatoms** and **radioalaria** (4) in the sea; **dinoflagellates** that live on pollution; and many others. A few protists, such as malaria, cause serious diseases.

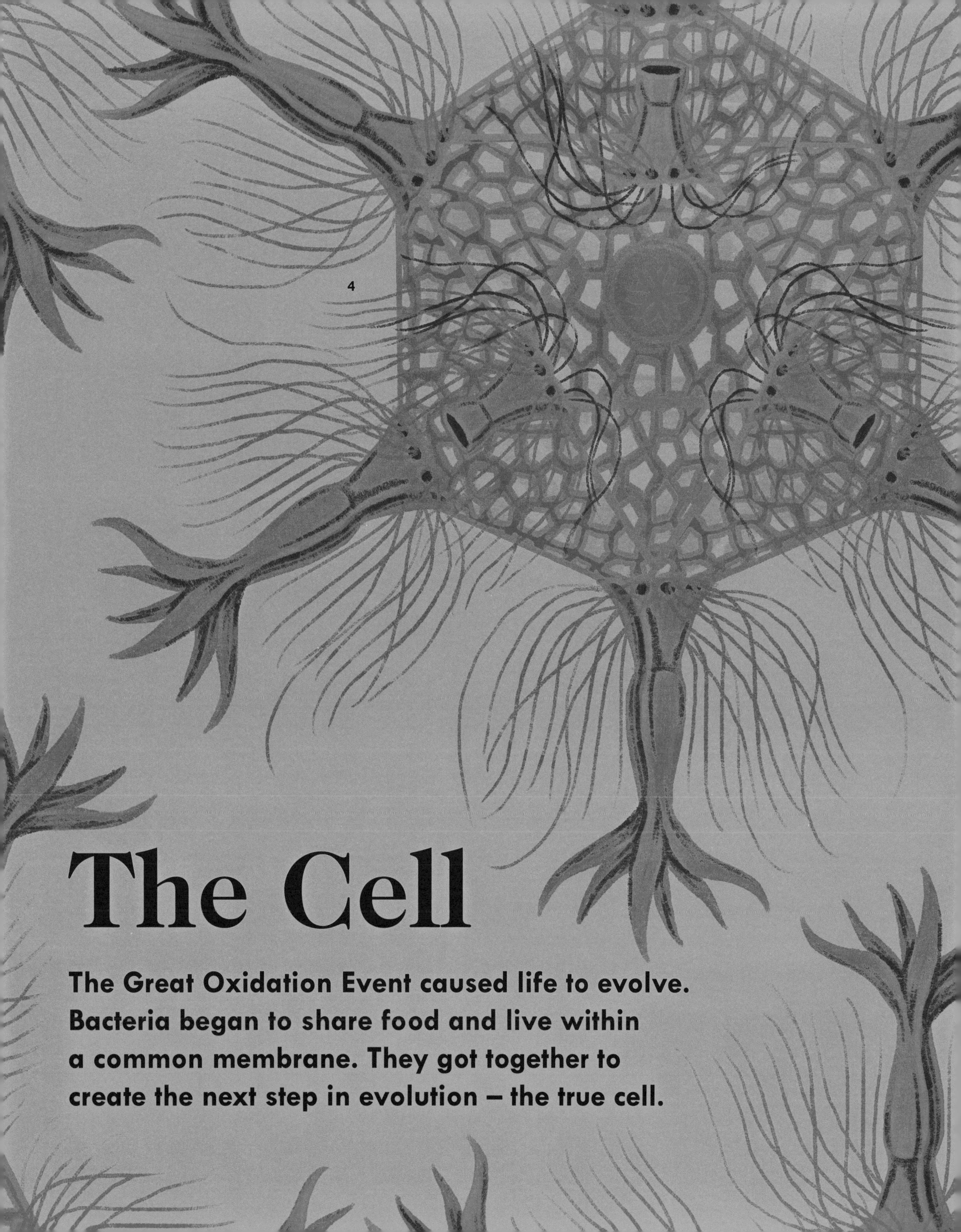

The Cell

The Great Oxidation Event caused life to evolve. Bacteria began to share food and live within a common membrane. They got together to create the next step in evolution – the true cell.

Eukaryote

Did you know that you are a eukaryote?

Some **eukaryotes** (such as you) have bodies that are made from many different cells working together. They are 'multicellular' creatures.

After the Great Oxidation Event, eukaryotes started to evolve and diversify. Multicellular creatures began to appear, like **Bangiomorpha** (1), a seaweed that looks a lot like seaweed today. **Ourasphaira** (2) was one of the earliest fungi.

There were stranger things. Some fossilized creatures that lived 2.1 billion years ago are hard to classify as seaweeds, fungi, or anything we know today. They could represent a kind of life – eukaryote, bacteria, or something completely different – that no longer exists today.

Eukaryotes evolved in a long period of relative peace, between 2.1 billion and 850 million years ago.

Then came a series of ice ages that led to another step along evolution's journey: the appearance of animals.

1. Bangiomorpha
2. Ourasphaira
3. Cell

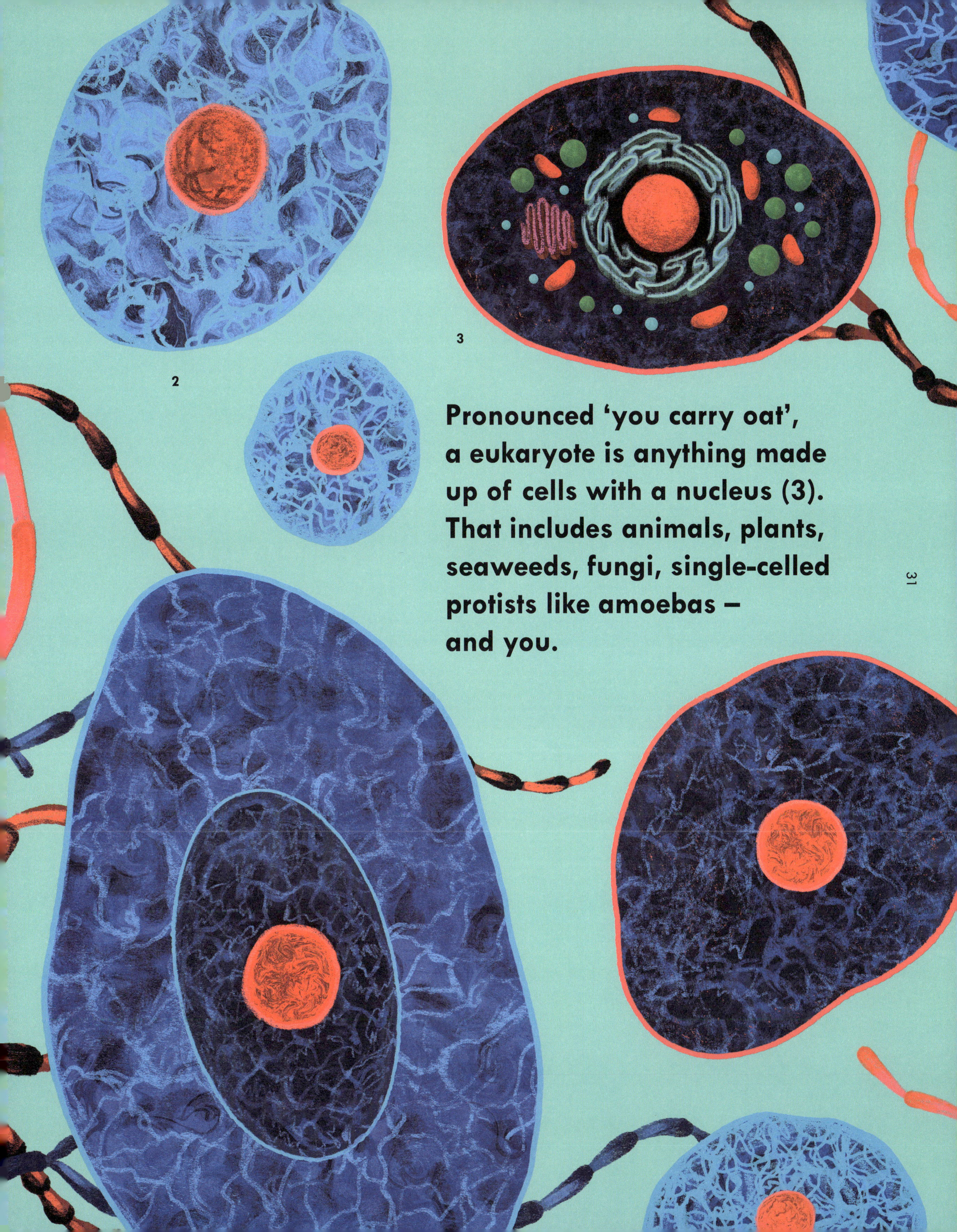

Pronounced 'you carry oat', a eukaryote is anything made up of cells with a nucleus (3). That includes animals, plants, seaweeds, fungi, single-celled protists like amoebas – and you.

Sponges

All animals need oxygen gas to breathe. They use oxygen to help release energy from the food they eat.

After oxygen levels spiked in the Great Oxidation Event, the amount of oxygen fell to 2 per cent of the atmosphere. Most animals need much more oxygen than that. Today, the atmosphere is 21 per cent oxygen. But some creatures had less need of oxygen – simple animals called sponges.

Sponges are hardly more than masses of cells loosely stuck together. They first appeared about 950 million years ago. Then, as now, they sat quietly on the ocean floor, filtering bacteria from seawater. But the quiet habits of sponges were to change the world.

At the time, there was almost no oxygen in the ocean, apart from just under the surface. Here, seaweeds were busy creating food from sunlight with photosynthesis. The bodies of dead seaweeds and other creatures were immediately consumed by bacteria and fungi. They also consumed what little oxygen there was in the water. This made it impossible for animals to evolve.

Sponges changed everything. They sucked up the organic material that the bacteria and fungi would have consumed. They even ate the bacteria and fungi themselves. This allowed oxygen to build up in the water.

The amount of seawater filtered by one sponge in one day is small. But the action of billions of sponges over a hundred million years cleared the ocean of decay, setting the stage for life's next great evolutionary leap.

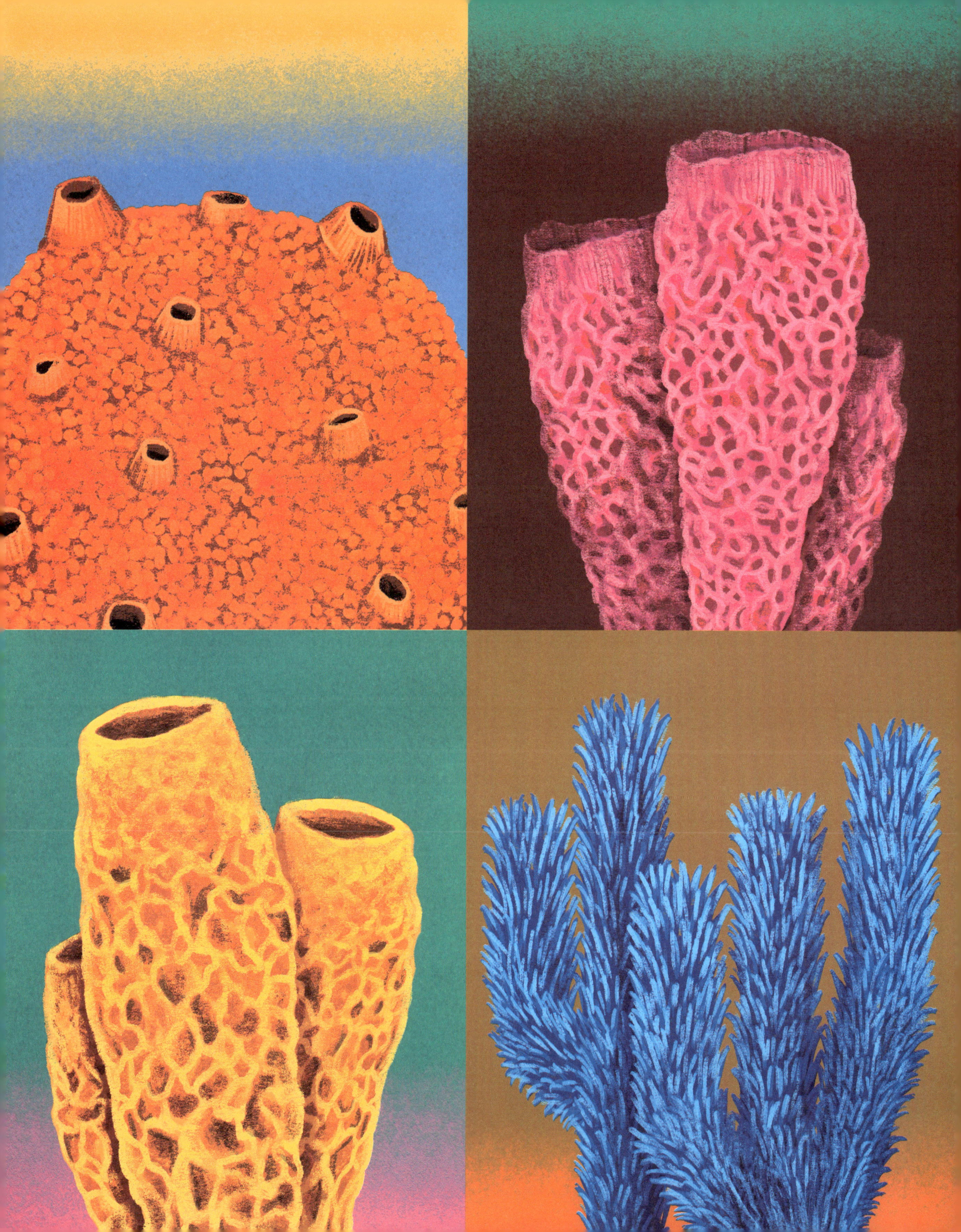

Rodinia

Around 3 billion years ago, the Earth was one enormous ocean.

Slowly, volcanic eruptions brought rocks to the surface. The first volcanic islands fused together to make larger pieces of land, which became continents. Two billion years later, the continents glued together into one huge land mass, a supercontinent called Rodinia.

The same forces that create supercontinents also tear them apart. The movement of the mantle under the Earth's crust forced apart the tectonic plates beneath Rodinia.

About 850 million years ago, the giant supercontinent was ripped into a series of smaller pieces that formed a ring around the Earth.

The weather got to work on the newly made continents. In the process of weathering, carbon dioxide in rainwater – carbonic acid – eats away at rocks, reacting with them chemically to create carbonate rocks. The result is that carbon dioxide gets tied up in rocks. The amount of carbon dioxide

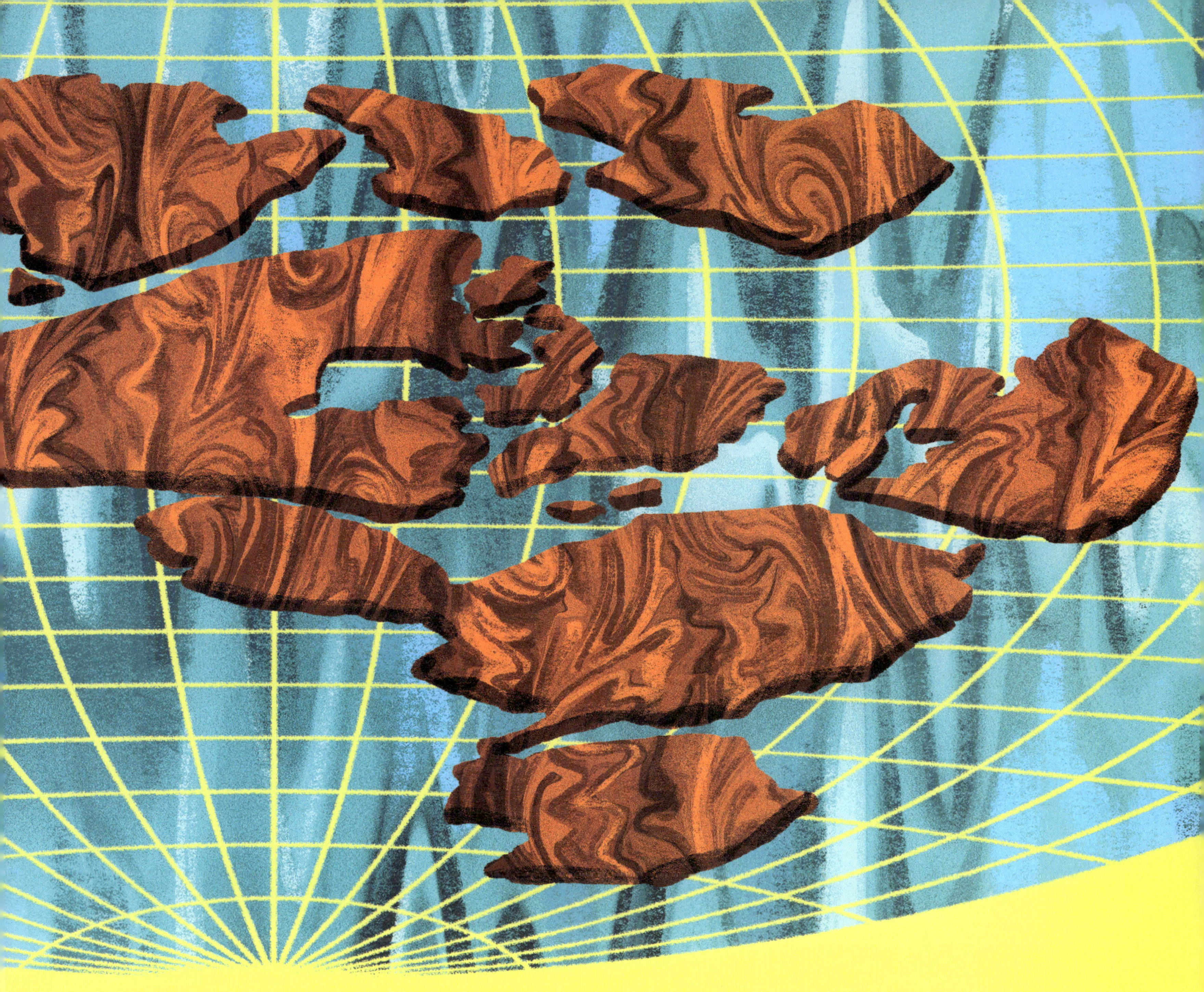

in the atmosphere falls. Without carbon dioxide in the atmosphere, the greenhouse effect weakens, and the Earth cools.

The break-up of Rodinia exposed more new rock to the atmosphere, increasing weathering. This pulled so much carbon dioxide out of the atmosphere that the Earth froze. The whole Earth was covered in ice for 80 million years. This was not quite as severe as the Ice Age at the time of the Great Oxidation Event, more than 2 billion years ago, which covered the Earth in ice for 300 million years. Although there was more land to soak up the carbon dioxide and cool the earth, the Sun was now much hotter.

The second Ice Age set the stage for the next leap in evolution – complex animal life.

1. *Tribrachidium* 2. *Ernietta* 3. *Haootia* 4. *Charnia* 5. *Cloudina* 6. *Yilingia* 7. *Dickinsonia* 8. *Fractofusus*

Ediacara

The first complex animals appeared 635–541 million years ago, in the Ediacaran Period. Ediacaran animals looked nothing like animals today.

Perhaps most curious were the rangeomorphs, like the fern-like Charnia (4). The worm-like Yilingia (6) lived late in the Ediacaran Period. It has been found fossilized at the end of the track it made on the ocean floor – caught in the act.

It is easy to imagine the pancake-like Dickinsonia (7) gliding over reefs in the same way that flatworms and sea slugs do today.

Fractofusus (8) lay like a plaited loaf on a plate. It reproduced by sending suckers from the mother creature, each one becoming a new, tiny plaited-loaf-shaped creature.

All the creatures from the Ediacaran Period were soft-bodied. They had no hard parts, like shells, teeth or armour, and lived in an ocean of peace and calm.

All that was about to change – and explosively.

Cambrian Explosion

The Cambrian Period began 541 million years ago. Once again, weathering scrubbed the surface of the land clear.

Nobody knows how or why, but the result was that huge amounts of rocks and minerals went into the sea.

What happened next was explosive: over a relatively short period of time, animals used the rocks and minerals in the sea to evolve hard teeth, shells and armour. This is known as the Cambrian Explosion.

After the peaceful Ediacaran Period, the Cambrian Period saw the evolution of animals that ate other animals: predators.

The earliest known example of an animal with a skeleton was called **Cloudina** (1). It looked like a stack of ice-cream cones, which probably contained a kind of worm. Fossils of Cloudina have been found with holes bored into them by predators.

Cloudina was soon followed by familiar animals like clams, and the ancient ancestors of insects, crabs, starfish and sea urchins.

Perhaps the most familiar Cambrian animals were the **trilobites** (2) – animals related to modern crustaceans and insects. They looked rather like woodlice. The sea thronged with them for millions of years. They finally became extinct at the end of the Permian Period, 252 million years ago. However, many other Cambrian animals appear very strange to us.

When animals evolved hard parts, they began to leave traces in the earth, and to burrow under the seafloor.

1. Cloudina 2. Trilobite

2

Burgess Shale

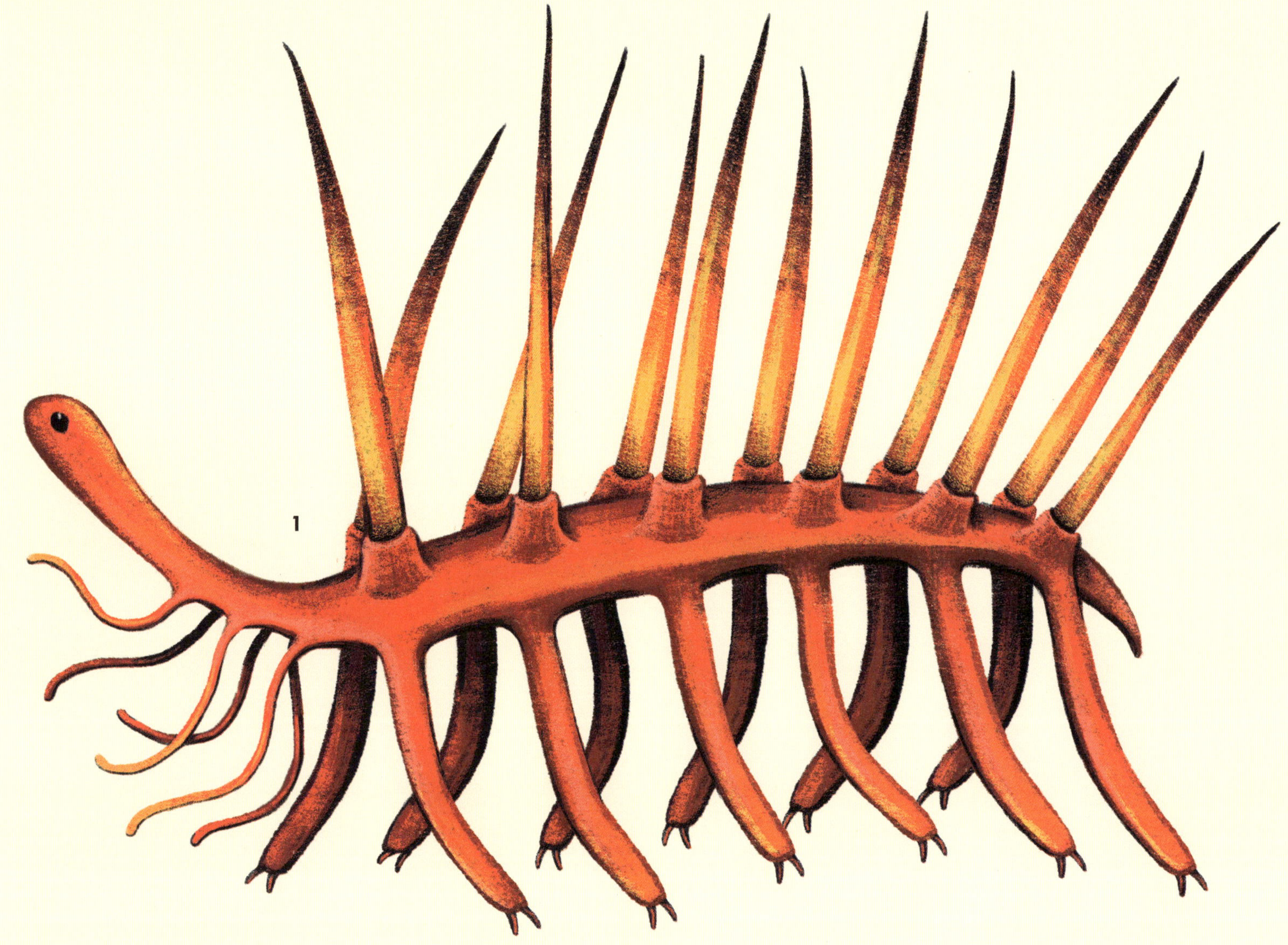

About 508 million years ago, there was a huge mudslide deep under the sea. Thousands of creatures were buried beneath the earth.

Millions of years later, the forces of plate tectonics brought this mud to rest among the highest peaks of British Columbia, Canada. The remains of the mudslide are called the Burgess Shale. They offer a marvellous glimpse of the weird and wonderful creatures living in the middle of the Cambrian Period.

1. Hallucigenia 2. Opabinia 3. Odontogriphus 4. Nectocaris 5. Wiwaxia

Hallucigenia (1) was a kind of worm with several pairs of long, fleshy legs and a row of huge spines on its back. It was related to the extremely strange **Opabinia** (2) – a shrimp-like swimmer with five eyes on stalks, and a long, hosepipe-like snout with jaws on the end.

Odontogriphus (3) looked like a cross between an airbed and a coffee grinder. It had a cheese-grater-like tongue called a radula. This shows it is in the same mollusc family as slugs, which also have a radula. They use theirs to eat leaves.

Nectocaris (4) was a streamlined mollusc relative, and is the earliest known member of the group called cephalopods (which today includes the squid and octopus).

Another mollusc relative was **Wiwaxia** (5), which looked like a slug covered in cornflakes.

Prowling above them all was **Anomalocaris** (see page 44), a metre-long swimming menace that stuffed anything it could catch with its fearsome pincers into its circular mouth.

Backbone

As the warm, shallow seas seethed with the spiky clatter of arthropod pincers, something was moving on the seafloor.

There, among the sand grains, lived a creature called **Saccorhytus**. It lived 540 million years ago in what is now China. No bigger than a pinprick and shaped like a potato, Saccorhytus sucked water in through a round mouth, filtered specks of food from the stream, and expelled the waste through two rows of slits.

This structure, called the pharynx, would turn out to be one of evolution's greatest successes.

Some animals evolved a suit of armour around the pharynx and became the **echinoderms** – spiny-skinned animals such as starfish and sea urchins.

Creatures like **vetulicolians** and **yunnanozoans** evolved to grow a tail at the back end of the pharynx. This was supported by a rod-like structure called the notochord.

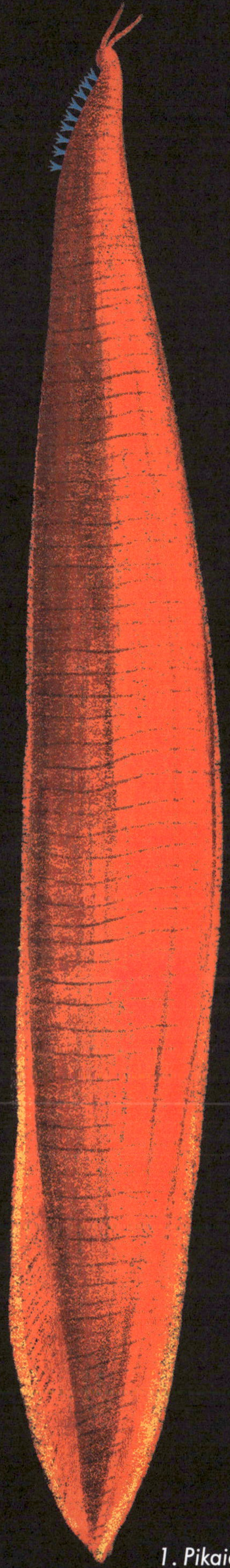

Pikaia (1), an animal that lived 508 million years ago in what is now Canada, also had a tail. Spending most of its time buried in sand, the tail was used for short, rapid journeys if danger threatened. Modern animals called **lancelets** are similar.

Tails and notochords were a huge evolutionary success. Tails helped creatures swim away from danger and far and wide for food. Notochords turned swimming into a way of life. The notochord became the backbone, and the pharynx evolved into gills over millions of years.

A creature had evolved that would pave the way for all vertebrates, like dinosaurs, mammals, and eventually, humans.

1. Pikaia

1
2
1
3

First Fish

Unlike Pikaia or lancelets, the earliest vertebrates had a head, with a brain inside a skull.

This was connected to a pair of eyes above a central mouth. The body was split into a series of V-shaped blocks of muscle, which you can see in any fish today. These would contract on each side, bending the animal into curves. The muscles were anchored against the notochord, which would become the backbone.

Metaspriggina (1) was one of the very first fish. It was soon joined by others, like **Haikouichthys** (2).

Although we call them the first fish, they were not very fish-like. The mouth was a hole with no jaws. There were no paired fins. The gills were simple pores, just rows of holes on each side of the head.

These early fish were more like lampreys and hagfish, which can be found in the ocean today. Like Metaspriggina and Haikouichthys, these animals have neither jaws nor paired fins.

There is something else these early fish lacked too – unusual for Cambrian animals. They had no scales, nor armour. They had to swim quickly to avoid Cambrian predators such as the spiky, spiny and very scary **Anomalocaris** (3).

1. Metaspriggina 2. Haikouichthys 3. Anomalocaris

Armour

For millions of years, every living creature was soft. There were no bones on Earth.

But at the end of the Cambrian Period, fish started to grow a kind of armour, made from a new substance – bone. The armour was thick around the jawless head, allowing the tail to move freely. The armour of most other creatures, such as molluscs, arthropods and echinoderms, is made of calcium carbonate. Bone is made of a different substance called calcium phosphate.

Armoured fish filled the seas from the Cambrian Period until the end of the Devonian Period, around 200 million years later. They came in an amazing variety of shapes and sizes. Collectively, armoured jawless fish are known as **ostracoderms**.

Some of these early fish, such as **thelodonts** (1), grew a suit of chain-mail-like scales. Some others, like **Tujiaaspis** (4), were covered in armour and grew a strangely shaped head shield. Stranger still were the **pituriaspids** (6), with their head shields and sword-like snouts.

None of these fish had jaws, so they were not very good hunters. They survived by grubbing for worms on the seafloor. They were prey for larger animals, such as the fearsome **eurypterids** – relatives of scorpions with sharp pincers and big goggling eyes. Some of these animals could grow to two metres long or more. Perhaps fish evolved their armour in response to the eurypterid threat.

1. Thelodont 2. Pteraspis 3. Arandaspis 4. Tujiaaspis 5. Errivaspis 6. Pituriaspid

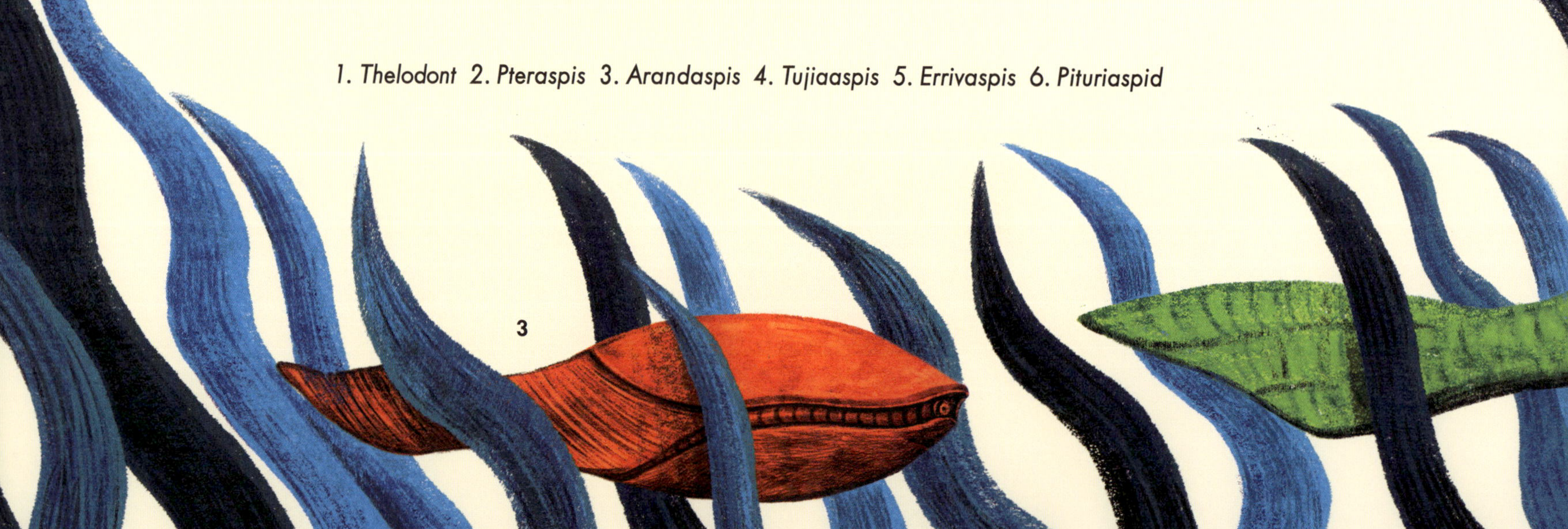

4
5
6

Jaws and Teeth

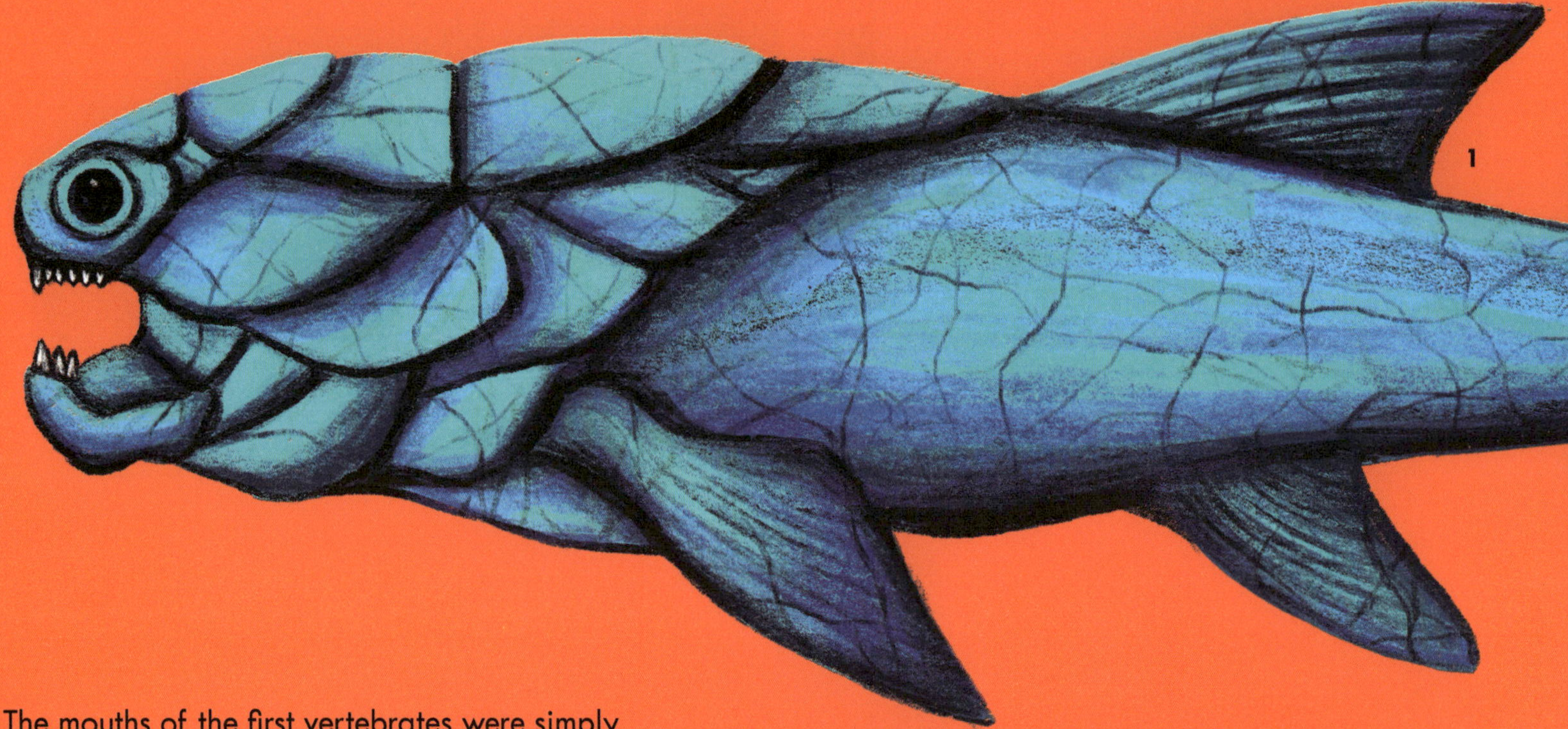

The mouths of the first vertebrates were simply holes at the front of the animal. The next big step in evolution was jaws – hinged sections with teeth that could chomp up and down. The first vertebrates with jaws were armoured fish called **placoderms**, which evolved in the Silurian Period, around 440 million years ago.

Some placoderms were less heavily armoured, while some became large and fierce. One, **Dunkleosteus** (1), grew to nearly 9 metres long and weighed 4 tonnes. It was the terror of the ocean. Placoderms all became extinct at the end of the Devonian Period, around 350 million years ago.

Placoderms shared the oceans with three other kinds of jawed fish. There were the **acanthodians** (2) or 'spiny sharks'.

Second were the true sharks, such as **Cladoselache** (3). They had tough bony scales, with skeletons made of soft cartilage (like the tip of your nose). Sharks have remained essentially the same since they evolved 443 million years ago.

Last were the bony fish. Like sharks, they had a skeleton, but made of bone. Most fish today – from seahorses and goldfish to the cod with your chips – are called 'ray-finned' bony fish. Their paired fins are attached directly to the body. The earliest well-known bony fish is **Guiyu** (4). Guiyu was not a ray-finned but a lobe-finned bony fish. It held its fins away from the body, like little arms and legs.

It's hard to imagine life without a mouth. Breathing and eating would be much more difficult.

1. Dunkleosteus
2. Acanthodian
3. Cladoselache
4. Guiyu

Walking

By the end of the Devonian Period (359 million years ago), the land was covered with forests.

Today, lobe-finned fish such as Guiyu are rare. In the Silurian (444–419 million years ago) and Devonian Periods (419–359 million years ago), they were much more common. Some evolved into **tetrapods**: vertebrates that live on land. Tetrapods include all amphibians, reptiles, birds and mammals, including you.

In the Devonian Period, a group of predatory lobe-finned fish called **elpistostegalians** evolved. They prowled shallow rivers and ponds. Unlike most fish, which are flattened from side to side, they were flattened from top to bottom, like alligators. They could breathe air and looked like giant newts – except that they had fins at the ends of their legs.

1. *Ichthyostega*

The earliest true tetrapods include **Acanthostega** and **Ichthyostega** (1). Acanthostega had eight toes on each limb but could never have survived on land for long. It had fish-like gills and its legs were more like flippers, best for swimming. Ichthyostega, with seven toes on each leg, might have flopped around on land like a seal.

The land that these early tetrapods walked upon was already rich with life. Lichens and algae had already started to live in freshwater 1.2 billion years ago. Small plants, such as **Cooksonia,** clothed the land in green.

There were trees such as **Archaeopteris**, and giant reed-like plants called **cladoxylopsids.** The ground swarmed with arthropods, including early relatives of spiders. Giant sea scorpions searched on land for fishy prey that had tried to escape by evolving legs.

By the early Carboniferous Period (about 340 million years ago), tetrapods had diversified into a range of forms that lived on land but laid their eggs in water, like frogs and newts do today. One of these was **Eucritta melanolimnetes** – which means 'The Creature from the Black Lagoon'.

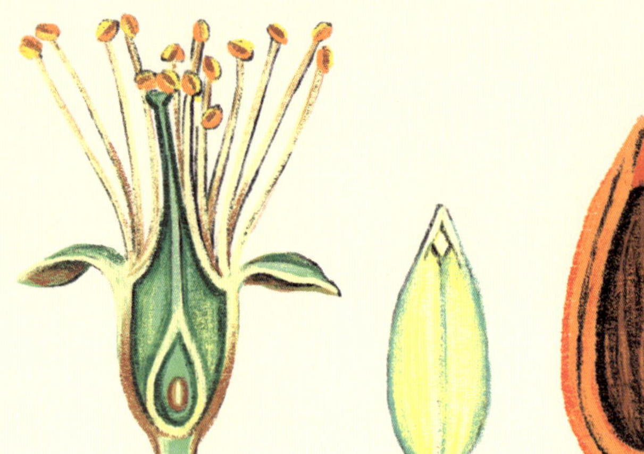

In the Carboniferous and early Permian Periods (from about 359 to roughly 252 million years ago) grew the greatest rainforests ever seen on Earth.

The trees would have looked strange to us. Scale trees, or clubmosses, had tall trunks with green leaf-like scales all the way up, instead of bark. **Horsetails** had branches spaced much more regularly than trees today. In those days, the horsetail **Calamites** grew 20 metres tall. The clubmoss **Lepidodendron** soared 50 metres into the sky – as tall as the tallest forest trees today. The coal we use as fuel is the fossilized remains of ancient trees.

Photosynthesis uses carbon dioxide and releases oxygen. Ancient forests used so much carbon dioxide that the greenhouse effect was reduced. Once again, the Earth cooled and glaciers formed at the South Pole. But there was so much oxygen in the air that dragonflies grew to the size of seagulls. Millipedes as long as a small car crawled on the forest floor. With all that oxygen, forest fires were common.

Early amphibians, like frogs and newts today, needed to return to the water to breed. Their eggs were a tasty snack for any passing animal, making them vulnerable. Some amphibians evolved tough shells for their eggs, protecting them from predators. These were the first reptiles.

Early plants also gradually evolved a way to reproduce away from water: the seed. A seed is a tough capsule in which the embryo plant can develop (a lot like an egg). The earliest plants with seeds were the 'seed ferns'.

The first reptiles looked and behaved much like amphibians. Some, such as **Petrolacosaurus** and **Hylonomus**, would evolve into snakes, lizards, crocodiles, dinosaurs and birds. **Archaeothyris** was one of a group of reptiles called the **pelycosaurs**. The pelycosaurs would, one day, evolve into mammals.

Egg and Seed

Therapsids

For millions of years, there were no creatures capable of digesting plants.

Early reptiles flourished in the Permian Period (299–252 million years ago).

The pelycosaurs were among the earliest reptiles. They included the carnivore **Dimetrodon**. Unlike other reptiles, it had two kinds of teeth. The word 'Dimetrodon' means 'teeth in two sizes'. It used its teeth to fight with giant land-living amphibians, such as **Eryops**, that looked like a giant bullfrog with attitude.

Another pelycosaur was **Edaphosaurus** (1), which was among the first plant-eating reptiles. Plants, unlike other kinds of prey, don't run away. However, they are tough to chew and digest. The first herbivores were giant insects with three pairs of wings – the **palaeodictyoptera**. Reptiles were late to the vegetarian party.

Pelycosaurs didn't survive. They were succeeded by their descendants, the **therapsids**. These evolved into a huge range of forms, from plant-eating creatures with tusks, such as **Aulacephalodon** (2), to meat-eating gorgonopsians like **Inostrancevia** (3), with huge pointy teeth like sabre-toothed tigers. Therapsids ranged from mole-sized burrowers to animals the size of hippos or elephants.

But the therapsid world came to a sudden end when, about 252 million years ago, more than 70 per cent of animals on land and 95 per cent in the sea were wiped out. A supervolcano in southern China, followed by an even larger one in Siberia, released enough carbon dioxide to raise the Earth's temperature by about 6 degrees Celsius.

Poisonous gases choked animals and plants. Chlorine-containing gases shredded the ozone layer. Acid rain destroyed the coral reefs and dissolved the calcium carbonate in animal shells. At any time in the past 500 million years, this was the closest that life has come to becoming completely extinct. Today, we call this extinction event the Great Dying.

But life would bounce back.

1. Edaphosaurus 2. Aulacephalodon 3. Inostrancevia

Life kept evolving after the Great Dying.

For several million years in the early Triassic Period (about 250–200 million years ago), nine out of every ten land vertebrates was a **Lystrosaurus**. This pig-like therapsid evolved into a huge range of forms.

The Earth swarmed with weird reptiles. Perhaps the weirdest was the gliding **Sharovipteryx** (2). There was **Tanystropheus**, with a neck longer than its tail and body combined. Many reptiles went back to the sea, like the dolphin-like **ichthyosaurs**. **Shonisaurus** was the largest ocean-dwelling reptile that ever lived.

Dinosaurs

Many animals we see today originated from this time, including turtles, frogs and mammals. But the later Triassic Period really belonged to the **archosaurs**, or 'ruling reptiles' (like the flying pterosaurs). And, of course, the **dinosaurs**.

Dinosaurs first appeared about 245 million years ago, and went on to dominate the earth for the next 180 million years. Although some were small and feathery, many grew to enormous sizes. **Patagotitan** (1) grew to 37 metres and weighed 55 tonnes. Giant herbivores were hunted by enormous carnivores such as **Tyrannosaurus**.

Alongside flowers, flower-feeding insects began to evolve, such as wasps, ants, bees and butterflies. They spread pollen, helping the flowers to grow.

The age of the dinosaurs came to a crashing end with an asteroid, which hit what is now Mexico 66 million years ago. The force of the impact destroyed huge swathes of land, ignited wildfires, and thick clouds blotted out the Sun.

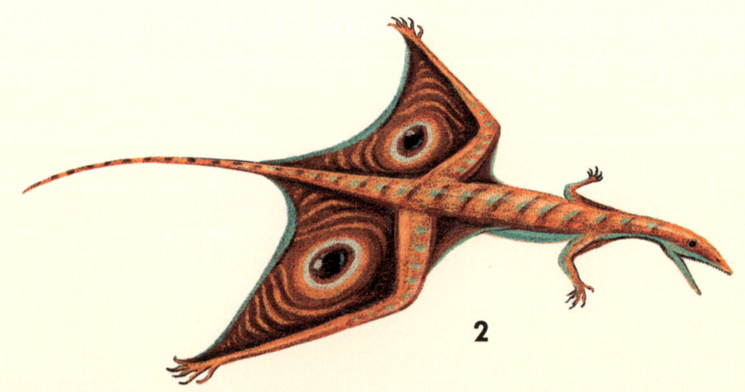

1. Patagotitan 2. Sharovipteryx

The later years of the dinosaurs were garlanded with a new arrival in the world – the first flowers.

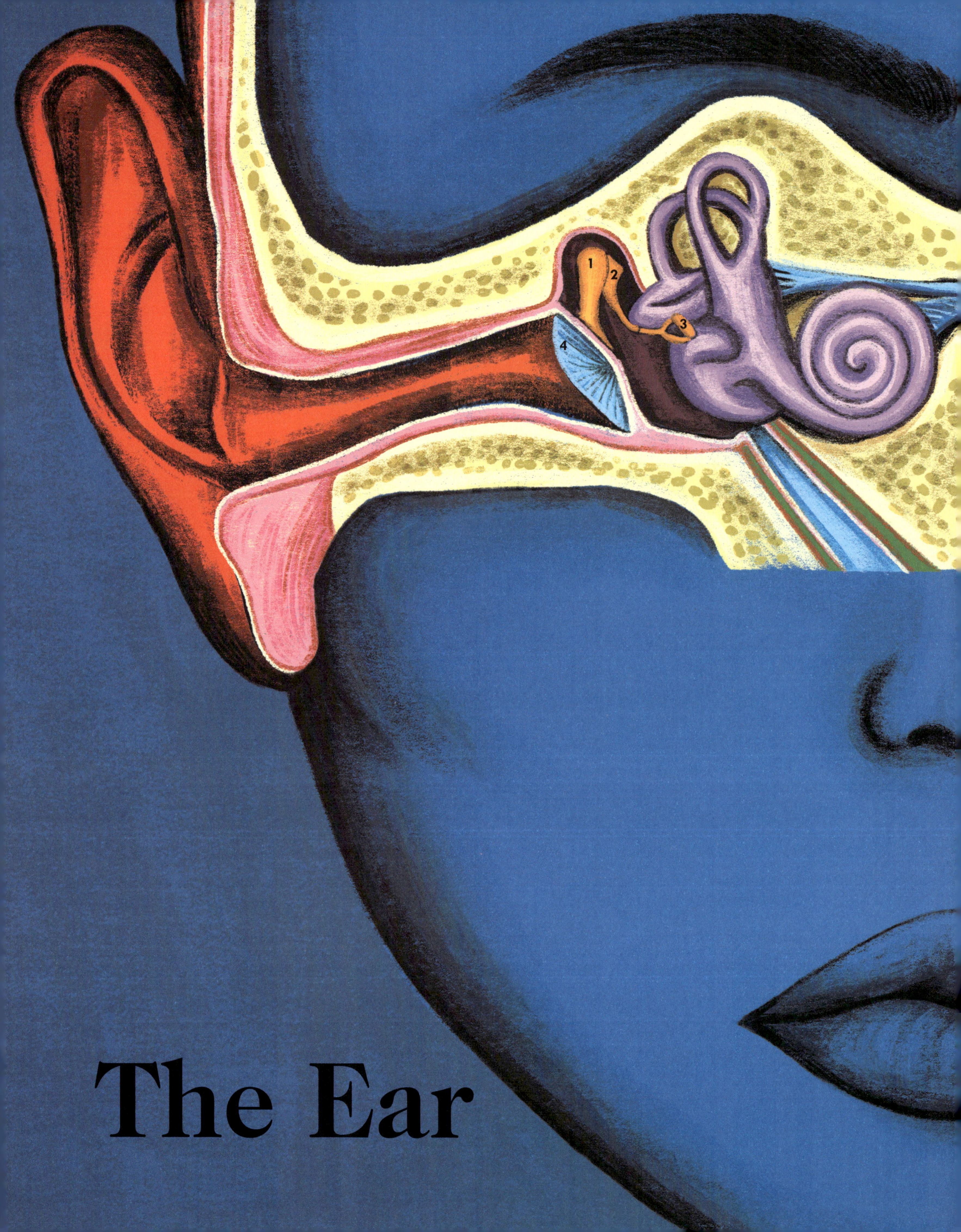

The Ear

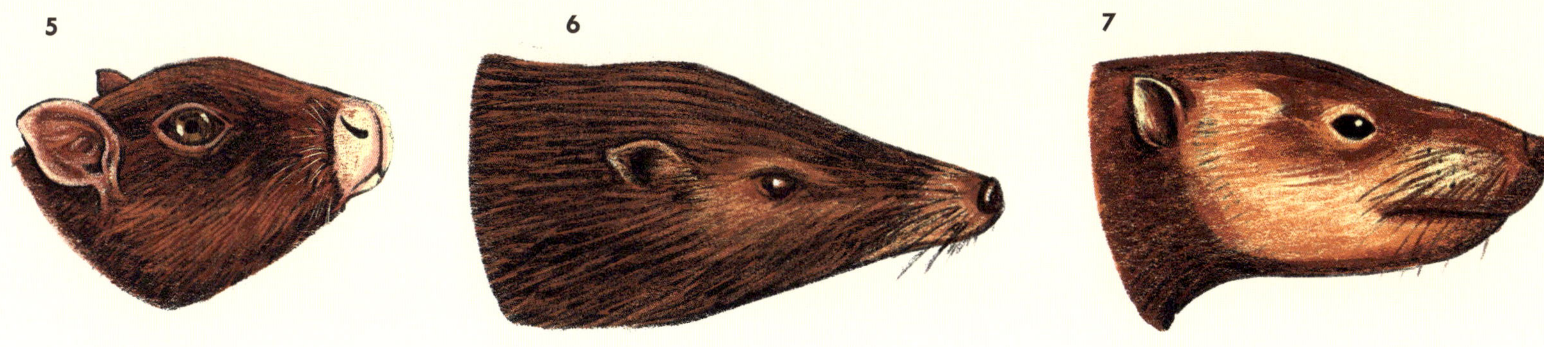

While dinosaurs ruled the day, mammals roamed at night, hunting insects. Their ancestors were therapsids called **cynodonts**. Cynodonts evolved to be smaller and furrier, with whiskers, and became the first mammals.

Being active at night meant that hearing was much more important for mammals than sight. The ears of land vertebrates had always worked the same way. Sound hitting the eardrum reached the inner ear via a single bone, called the stirrup bone. This is how reptiles and birds hear to this day.

But in mammals, the stirrup is joined by two other tiny bones: the hammer (1) and the anvil (2). These were once at the back of the jaw. The joint of the jaw is close to the ear (you can check this on your own head). As mammals evolved to become smaller, the bones at the back of the jaw became tiny and squashed together. Eventually, they came to rest inside the ear, between the stirrup (3) and the eardrum (4).

Mammals like bats, whales, and even cats and dogs can hear sounds far too high for birds to hear.

The result was a transformation. The chain of three bones made sounds louder. It became easier for mammals to hear high-pitched noises.

While dinosaurs thundered over the Earth, mammals evolved into at least twenty different groups. **Vilevolodon** (5) was a glider, swooping among the treetops millions of years before birds evolved. Plump **Castorocauda** (6) weighed 800 grams and had a beaver-like tail, perfect for swimming. Badger-sized **Repenomamus** (7) was a hunter – its prey was dinosaur eggs and babies.

The asteroid that wiped the dinosaurs from the Earth also drove most mammals to extinction. But not all.

When the dinosaurs were gone, it was the turn of mammals to emerge into the light.

1. Malleus (hammer) 2. Incus (anvil) 3. Stapes (stirrup) 4. Eardrum
5. Vilevolodon 6. Castorocauda 7. Repenomamus

Mammals

The asteroid that destroyed the dinosaurs turned the Earth into a harsh place.

Clouds of dust blotted out the light, and the Earth was plunged into a winter that lasted for years. Many plants died, and animals starved. But life hung on.

Mammals evolved into many new forms after the dinosaurs became extinct. Within a few million years, some mammals had evolved that were as large as rhinos. By the Eocene Period, around 55 million years ago, mammals had evolved into most of their modern groups – although they would have looked very different. Animals such as **Diacodexis** (1) were small and rabbity, but have evolved into **ungulates** like cows and sheep.

1. *Diacodexis*
2. *Paraceratherium*
3. *Hispanotherium*
4. *Elasmotherium*
5. *Icaronycteris*

5

The Earth at this time was a hothouse planet, covered in jungle. Some early ungulates returned to the water and became whales. The transition from dog-like **Pakicetus** to the sea-serpent-like **Basilosaurus** took just 8 million years. The first bats, such as **Icaronycteris** (5), took to the skies.

For a long time, South America and Africa were island continents, each with its own unique mammals. In South America, armadillos and sloths grazed alongside weird ungulates not seen anywhere else. All were hunted by ferocious sabre-toothed **marsupials**. In Africa, small insect-eating mammals evolved into elephants, hyraxes and dugongs.

Around 30 million years ago, the Earth began to cool. The jungles were no more. Ungulates evolved to graze a new kind of plant – grass. In the Oligocene Epoch (34–23 million years ago), rhinos, elephants and horses munched the plains. Early primates such as **Notharctus** were tiny and tropical, but by the Miocene Epoch (23–5.3 million years ago) they had evolved into monkeys and apes.

4

3

Primates are a group of mammals that includes lemurs, monkeys and apes – as well as humans.

Monkeys are small and generally have tails. Apes (like gorillas, chimpanzees and orangutans) tend to be larger, and do not have tails. Today, there are many more species of monkey than ape. But during the Miocene Epoch, apes were much more common. Some evolved to stand upright.

Walking upright became a habit for one particular group of apes – the **hominins**.

By the Pliocene Epoch, 5.3–2.6 million years ago, the world became cooler and drier. Forests withered, leaving huge stretches of grassland. Hominins became more successful than the forest-loving apes. **Australopithecus** was the first hominin to walk as modern humans do. It also made stone tools.

Apes

Australopithecus evolved into two very different hominins. **Paranthropus** was a vegetarian with huge teeth for munching roots and nuts. They died out about 600,000 years ago. The other was **Homo**. At first, Homo was much like Australopithecus – eating just about anything.

About 2.5 million years ago, the world's climate became even drier and colder. Africa produced a new kind of hominin, the more carnivorous **Homo erectus**. It learned how to do two new things. The first was running over long distances, allowing it to chase its prey. Hunting meant that Homo erectus could eat fresh meat, rather than scavenging for leftovers.

The second was how to use fire, allowing food to be cooked. Cooking kills germs, and makes food more nutritious. Homo erectus now had enough food to develop a larger brain.

Homo erectus was the first hominin to leave Africa and take over the world.

Homo Erectus

Two million years ago, huge herds of antelope and other game spread over the grasslands that covered Africa, Europe and Asia. Homo erectus followed them. As Homo erectus spread, it evolved.

Homo erectus (1) adapted to the deepening cold of Europe by evolving into a tough, hardy creature – **Neanderthals** (2). These hominins spent a lot of time in caves underground, away from the wind and cold. Deep in a cave 176,000 years ago, Neanderthals made structures of broken rock and bear bones. Nobody knows why. These are the oldest known structures built by hominins. Neanderthals also buried their dead, garlanding them with flowers.

1. Homo erectus 2. Neanderthal 3. Homo luzonensis
4. Homo floresiensis 5. Homo sapiens

The descendants of Homo erectus looked up, as well as down. Travelling over Asia, they noticed the high mountains, and climbed them. And as they climbed, they evolved into a tough species of mountaineers, called the **Denisovans**.

At least two groups of Homo erectus migrated to islands, where they evolved into strange new forms.

Many animals on islands evolve over time to get smaller in size. On the Philippines, tiny **Homo luzonensis (3)** hunted tiny rhinos. On the Indonesian island of Flores, hobbit-sized **Homo floresiensis (4)** hunted miniature elephants and giant rats, while battling Komodo dragons of enormous size.

Meanwhile, back in Africa, another new species was evolving. This was the first hint of our own species, **Homo sapiens (5)**.

Homo Sapiens

The earliest signs of Homo sapiens are 315,000 years old. But these early people were not very much like we are today.

Early Homo sapiens interbred with other hominins in Africa, as well as Neanderthals and Denisovans in Europe and Asia.

As the Ice Age went on, Homo sapiens nearly died out. About 130,000 years ago, the climate became milder and our species spread throughout southern and eastern Africa. Humans reached Australia around 60,000 years ago. Around 45,000 years ago, Homo sapiens spread into Europe. The last Neanderthals died out. At about this time, all other species of hominin on Earth also became extinct.

At the same time, Homo sapiens began to make art. Beautiful paintings of people and animals found in caves in Europe and Indonesia date from this time.

Part of the success of Homo sapiens can be put down to two quirks of human reproduction. First, human babies take many years to grow up. This created a new phase of life – childhood. Second, unlike most other mammals, human females can live for many years after they stop having babies. This created a new group not seen among most other animals – grandparents.

Grandparents could help their children raise more children, and tell them stories. For Homo sapiens is a species that loves to tell stories to its children.

As far as we know, Homo sapiens is the only species that is conscious of its own place in the universe, and able to tell stories about it. Rather like the story of life on Earth in this book.

Homo sapiens is a phenomenon. About 10,000 years ago, humans started farming. They began settling down, instead of always roaming from place to place. Farming started in several different parts of the world at the same time. After that, human society began to grow at a staggering rate. The invention of metalwork, religions, technology, science and medicine followed.

A person born in 1903 – the year the first aeroplane flew – could easily have lived to witness the first people walking on the Moon in 1969. More than fifty years later, your phone has more computing power than the spacecraft that took them there.

Because of human inventions, most people live longer, healthier and more fulfilled lives than our ancestors did. Fifty years ago, only one in five children stayed in school after the age of twelve. Now it is one in two.

Human Explosion

Since the invention of farming, the population has expanded from a few million to more than 8 billion. Today, humans make up 36 per cent of the mass of mammals. With our domestic animals – cows and sheep, cats and dogs – we make up 96 per cent. All other mammals, from aardvarks to zebras, giraffes to elephants, make up the remaining 4 per cent.

Humans consume up to 40 per cent of all the energy that plants gather by photosynthesis. As a result of human activity, ecosystems and the climate are changing in dangerous and unpredictable ways.

But the rate of human population growth is slowing. The human population will most likely reach 10–11 billion in the 2060s. After that, it is predicted to fall. In 2100, the population of the Earth will probably be about the same as it is now, about 8 billion. Homo sapiens may be extinct in a few thousand years.

The Future

Life on Earth is ruled by just two things. One is the amount of carbon dioxide in the atmosphere, which is vital for plants to grow. The other is the amount of heat coming from the Sun.

Over billions of years, the amount of carbon dioxide in the atmosphere is falling. To be sure, it has its ups and downs. Because of human activity, there is more carbon dioxide in the atmosphere now than there has been for at least 3 million years. This has led to rapid climate change and dangerously unpredictable weather all over the world. It is a serious threat to human life and the welfare of the other species with which we share our planet.

But over the longest timescales, the amount of carbon dioxide in the atmosphere is falling. The reason is that over millions of years, the Earth is creating more land. New land absorbs more carbon dioxide than can be produced by volcanoes.

New rocks will become rarer – volcanoes, rarer still. The great heat engines at the centre of the Earth are cooling down. They may stop altogether in about a billion years. This means that much less carbon dioxide will be generated to replace that which is absorbed by new rocks. The time will come when the amount of carbon dioxide will become too small to feed plants.

The Sun, too, is changing. One reason the Earth could be covered in ice for 300 million years during the Great Oxidation Event, 2.1–2.4 billion years ago, is because the Sun was much cooler than it is now. The Earth still has ice ages, but they are much less severe because the Sun is hotter. One day, the Sun will become too hot for life on the surface to survive.

But don't panic. None of this will happen for another 1 billion years. Between now and then, life on Earth will produce many more surprises. What will future animals and plants look like? How many species will outlast humans on Earth?

Their fate is in our hands, now.

Glossary

Algae – simple plants such as seaweed that mostly live in water. Although most are single cells, some, such as giant kelp, are enormous.

Amniote – an animal that lays eggs with a waterproof shell. Amniotes include reptiles and birds. Most mammals, like us, do not lay eggs but are also amniotes, as they evolved from reptiles.

Amphibian – an animal that lives on land but reproduces in water, like frogs, toads and newts.

Ancestor – a creature from which others descend. Finding a true ancestor as a fossil is very difficult. It's easier to say that creatures found as fossils are relatives, such as cousins, of creatures living today.

Arthropod – an animal with jointed legs and a skeleton on the outside, such as flies, beetles, spiders and crabs.

Asteroid – a potato-shaped rock that orbits the Sun in space, varying in size from large pebbles to small planets.

Atmosphere – the layer of air that surrounds a planet such as the Earth.

Atom – a tiny particle of matter. Far too small to be seen even with most microscopes, the shapes and sizes of atoms give substances their basic properties.

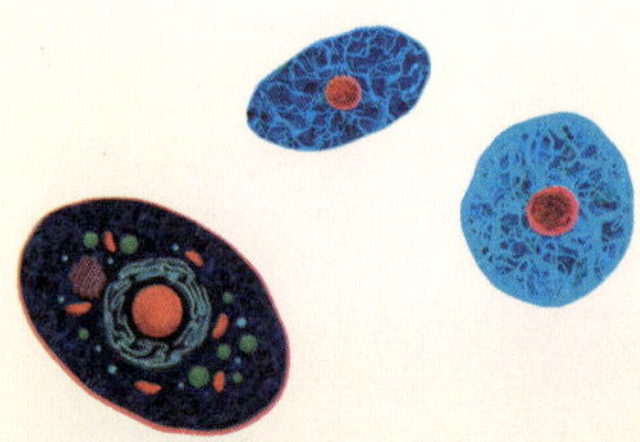

Bacteria – very small living things made from single cells.

Biofilm – a colony of different kinds of bacteria.

Cell – the fundamental building block of most large living things such as yourself.

Cephalopod – a group of molluscs that today includes squid and octopus.

Climate – the warmth or coolness of the atmosphere, determined by sunshine, the sea, and the shape of the land.

Comet – an asteroid-like body that orbits the Sun in space, but which contains a lot of water, gas and dust that streams out like a tail when it gets close to the Sun.

Continental Drift – the very slow process in which continents, carried on tectonic plates, move across the Earth's surface, sometimes sticking together into huge supercontinents such as Rodinia or Pangaea, at other times splitting apart.

Crust – the rocky outermost layer of the solid Earth.

Crustacean – a group of arthropods (see above) that includes crabs, lobsters, shrimps and woodlice.

Cynodont – one of a group of therapsids that were close relatives of mammals, and from which mammals evolved. Many cynodonts had fur and whiskers, like mammals. They lived in the Permian and Triassic periods.

Dinosaur – one of a large group of reptiles that lived from about 220 million to 65 million years ago.

DNA (deoxyribonucleic acid) – the substance inside all cells that determines their genetic heritage.

Echinoderm – a spiny-skinned sea creature, such as a starfish, sea urchin or sea cucumber.

Embryo – the young stage of a creature while it is developing in the egg, womb, or, if a plant, inside the seed.

Eukaryote – a creature such as an animal, plant, alga or fungus that has large, complex cells.

Evolution – the process by which creatures slowly change over many generations.

Extinction – the process in which an entire species, or larger group pf animals or plants, disappears. Extinctions happen all the time. Sometimes many creatures go extinct all together because of some catastrophe, such as a supervolcano or asteroid or comet hitting the Earth.

Fossil – the remains of a living creature preserved in rock. Most fossils are the hard parts such as bones or shells. Occasionally, soft parts such as skin, hair, feathers and internal organs are preserved. Fossils may include things animals left behind such as footprints or poo.

Fungi – a group of eukaryotes that includes mushrooms, toadstools, mould and mildew.

Gene – made of DNA, genes define the qualities of living beings, such as eye colour or seed shape.

Gills – delicate frond- or sheet-like structures that help water creatures such as fish to breathe.

Gravity – a force of nature in which bodies of matter attract one another.

Herbivore – an animal that eats plants.

Hominin – a member of the human family, such as Australopithecus or Homo erectus. All are extinct except for our own species, Homo sapiens.

Ice Age – a period of thousands or millions of years in which large parts of the Earth are frozen.

Invertebrate – all animals without backbones.

Lichen – a living creature made from a very close relationship between an alga and a fungus.

Magma – rock that is so hot that it flows like liquid.

Mammal – a vertebrate with hair that suckles its young with milk, and almost always carries the young. Includes many familiar animals, such as dogs, cats, cows, horses, sheep, bats, mice, elephants, whales, and ourselves.

Mantle – the layer of rock inside the Earth between the outer crust and the inner core.

Marsupial – a kind of mammal that raises its young in a pouch on its body.

Meteor – a small space rock that falls into the Earth's atmosphere, often creating a bright 'shooting star'.

Meteorite – the rocky remains of a meteor once it hits the ground.

Mineral – a non-living substance, sometimes found as crystals or gemstones, that are the main ingredients of rocks.

Mollusc – an animal such as a clam, snail or slug. Although many have hard shells, some, such as squid, have an internal shell. A few, such as the octopus, have no shell, and are among the cleverest animals.

Natural selection – the driving force through which living things constantly adapt to their surroundings and so evolve.

Nucleus (atomic) – the small, central part of an atom.

Nucleus (cell) – the particle in a eukaryotic cell that contains the genetic material DNA.

Pelycosaur – one of a group of reptiles that lived in the Permian period. They included the 'sail-backed' reptiles **Dimetrodon** and **Edaphosaurus**.

Photosynthesis – the process in which green plants harvest sunshine, carbon dioxide and water and create sugars and other substances.

Planet – a body of matter that forms in orbit around a star. Planets are spherical, larger than asteroids and smaller than stars. Our Earth is a planet.

Plant – a group of eukaryotes that usually stay rooted in a single place.

Plate Tectonics – the process in which segments of the Earth's crust split into regions that move independently on the underlying mantle. Earthquakes and volcanoes happen when tectonic plates bump into one another.

Predator – a creature that hunts other creatures on which it then feeds.

Prey – the victims of predators.

Primate – a group of mammals that includes monkeys, apes and humans.

Protein – the substance from which living creatures are made.

Protist – a single-celled eukaryote such as an amoeba, a paramecium, a dinoflagellate, or a malaria parasite.

Reptile – one of a group of animals that today includes snakes, lizards, turtles and crocodiles. Dinosaurs, birds and mammals evolved from reptiles. Extinct reptiles include pelycosaurs, therapsids, the flying pterosaurs, the swimming ichthyosaurs and many others.

Rock – a collection of minerals fused into a single substance, such as granite, sandstone, or chalk.

Soil – the substance that forms on the Earth's surface through the action of plants, bacteria, fungi and small animals.

Star – a gigantic ball of gas that becomes so dense that the atoms in its centre fuse together and create heat and light.

Supernova – an explosion created when a giant star (much bigger than our own Sun) runs out of fuel, collapses and explodes.

Tectonic plate – a piece of the Earth's crust.

Tetrapod – a vertebrate that has four legs with fingers and toes.

Therapsid – one of a group of reptiles that evolved from pelycosaurs and lived in the Permian and Triassic periods. Mammals evolved from a group of therapsids called cynodonts. They included Aulacephalodon and Inostrancevia.

Ultraviolet or UV – a form of light that is invisible to us, but contains a lot of energy.

Vertebrate – an animal with an internal skeleton, or backbone.

Author's Note

A few years ago, I wrote a book called *A (Very) Short History of Life on Earth*. In it, I told the story of the Earth from its beginning, right through to the end of life, maybe a billion years from now.

Most people really liked the book, except for one thing – there were no pictures. This book is my response to the many requests I have had for an illustrated version. The text, though, is completely new, written specially for this version. I thank Helen Weir at Two Hoots for her editorial guidance, helping me get this new text into shape. Many other people helped along the way including Ravindra Mirchandani, Steve Brusatte and Jill Grinberg, and my family.

Of course, my biggest thanks must go to Raxenne Maniquiz for her wonderful illustrations. I hope you'll agree that they are marvellous. They remind me of a book I read as a small child called *The First Days of the Earth*. That was a long time ago, and you can't get it any more. If you are looking for more books like this, there are many more to explore. One of my favourites is *Life Before Man* by Z. V. Spinar and Zdenek Burian. This was originally published in 1972, and there have been several editions since. The earlier ones, if you can find them, are the best. If you want more about dinosaurs, do look out for my own book *A Field Guide to Dinosaurs*, illustrated by Luis V. Rey.

H. G.

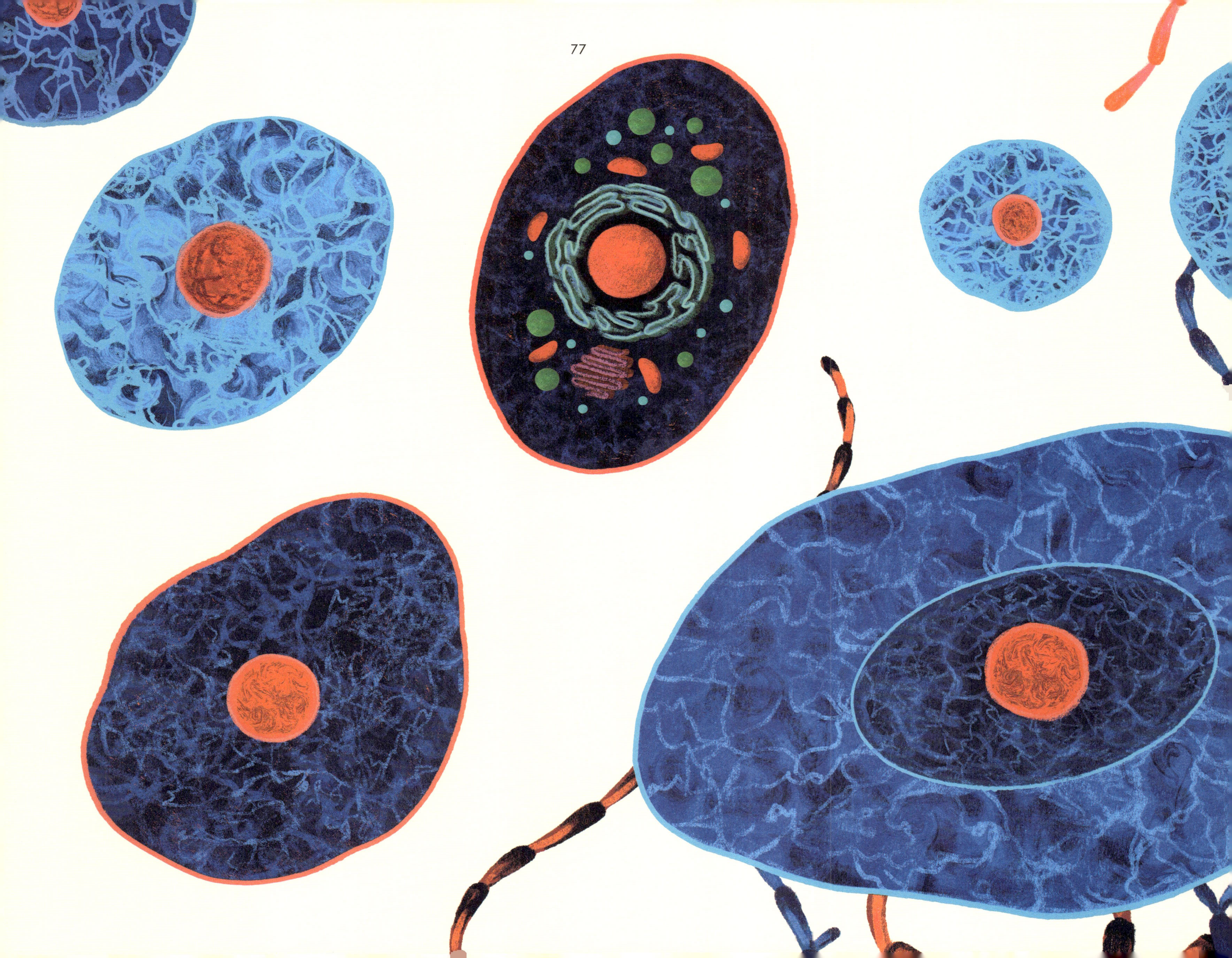